Georgia O'Keeffe was born on
a farm in Wisconsin in 1887.

When I was twelve years old,
I knew what I wanted—
to be an artist.

I've always known what I wanted....
When I was small
I played alone for hours and hours and hours.
I was satisfied to be all by myself.

I did things other people don't do.
When my sisters wore sashes—I didn't.
When my sisters wore stockings—I wore none.

MY NAME IS
Georgia

A PORTRAIT BY
Jeanette Winter

Voyager Books • Harcourt, Inc.

Orlando   Austin   New York   San Diego   London

For Paula Wiseman, with special thanks to Judythe Sieck

In making this portrait of Georgia O'Keeffe for young readers, I have tried to imagine her life as autobiography. Although the illustrations are my own, they have been done in homage to her art and include many of the images she often used. Except for those quotations of O'Keeffe herself that I have selected from published writings, referred to in the bibliography of sources that follows and indicated in the text by italics, the words are my own. —J. W.

Select Bibliography

Arrowsmith, Alexandra, and Thomas West, editors. *Two Lives: Georgia O'Keeffe and Alfred Steiglitz*. New York: HarperCollins Publishers/ Callaway Editions in association with the Phillips Collection, Washington, D.C., 1992.

Eisler, Benita. *O'Keeffe and Steiglitz: An American Romance*. New York: Doubleday, 1991.

Gherman, Beverly. *Georgia O'Keeffe: The Wideness and Wonder of Her World*. New York: Atheneum, 1986.

Hogrefe, Jeffrey. *O'Keeffe: The Life of an American Legend*. New York: Bantam Books, 1992.

Lisle, Laurie. *Portrait of an Artist: A Biography of Georgia O'Keeffe*. Albuquerque: University of New Mexico, 1986.

Giboire, Clive. *Lovingly, Georgia: The Complete Correspondence of Georgia O'Keeffe and Anita Pollitzer*. New York: Simon & Schuster, 1990.

O'Keeffe, Georgia. *Georgia O'Keeffe*. New York: Viking Press, 1976.

Peters, Sarah Whitaker. *Becoming O'Keeffe: The Early Years*. New York: Abbeville Press, 1991.

Robinson, Roxana. *Georgia O'Keeffe: A Life*. New York: Harper & Row, 1989.

From the Faraway Nearby, painted by Georgia O'Keeffe, 1937.
Georgia O'Keeffe: Arts and Letters. Washington, D.C.: The National Gallery of Art, 1987.

Braggiotti, Mary. "Her Worlds Are Many," *New York Post*, May 16, 1946.
Tompkins, Calvin. "The Rose in the Eye Looked Pretty Fine," *The New Yorker* (March 4, 1974): 40–66.
Willard, Charlotte. "Georgia O'Keeffe," *Art in America* (October 1963).

Copyright © 1998 by Jeanette Winter

www.hmhbooks.com

First Voyager Books edition 2003
Voyager Books is a trademark of Harcourt, Inc., registered in the United States of America and/or other jurisdictions.

The Library of Congress has cataloged the hardcover edition as follows:
Winter, Jeanette.
My name is Georgia: A portrait/Jeanette Winter.
p.   cm.
Summary: Presents, in brief text and illustrations, the life of the painter who drew much of her inspiration from nature.
1. O'Keeffe, Georgia. 1887–1986—Juvenile literature.   2. Artists—United States—Biography—Juvenile literature.
[1. O'Keeffe, Georgia, 1887–1986.   2. Artists.   3. Women—Biography.]   I. Title.
ND237.05W56   1998
759.13—dc21[B]   97-7087
ISBN 978-0-15-201649-4
ISBN 978-0-15-204597-5 pb

SCP   18   17   16
4500419669
Printed in China

And when my sisters wore braids—
I let my black hair fly.

I rode to town every Saturday to copy pictures
from the stack in the art teachers' cupboard.

At home, I looked out my window
and drew pictures of what I saw.

Maybe I could make something beautiful. . . .
At school in Chicago,
I drew from statues in the museum.

At school in New York,
I painted one still-life painting a day—every day.
At school, I painted my teachers' ideas.

But when school days were over,
I went out into the wide world
to discover my own ideas.

I went to the Texas plains,
the Wild West of my childhood books.
. . . you have never seen SKY—
it is wonderful.

. . . I walked into the sunset.

I felt the wind across the plains.

And I painted the sunset and the sky
and the wonderful loneliness and
emptiness of the place.
I painted day and night.

I worked till my head all felt light in the top.
I have things in my head that are
not like what anyone has taught me—
shapes and ideas.

But I bundled up my paintings
and went to New York City,
to be where other artists lived.

I walked down in the canyons of steel.

I lived high up in the clouds
and painted what I saw from my window.

But sometimes, what I saw from my window
was the *faraway,* calling me.

I painted a garden in the city.
I wanted everyone to see flowers
the way I saw them.

I looked closely at the flowers.

I painted a camellia.
I painted it BIG, so people would notice.

I painted a jack-in-the-pulpit.
I painted it BIG, so people would see.

I painted poppies and petunias and sunflowers
and jimsonweeds and irises and apple blossoms.
My garden bloomed, until everyone saw
the flowers the way I saw them.

But still, I looked to the sky.
The distance has always been calling me.

I went to the New Mexico desert.

So far away that no one ever comes . . .

I was satisfied to be all by myself.

It was too dry for the flowers to grow.
But there were bones.

I gathered the bones—
big bones, little bones, short bones, long bones,
a cow's skull, a horse's skull, a ram's skull—
and brought the bones home to paint.

One day I held one up against the sky
and saw the blue through that hole.
I painted what I saw.

I saw the sky—
and the red hills.
I walked in the hills at daybreak and twilight,
at noon and in starlight.

*I painted the arms of two red hills
reaching out to the sky and holding it.*

I painted the Pedernal mountain in the *faraway*.
I painted it over and over and over again.
And then again and again.

God told me if I painted that mountain enough,
he'd give it to me.

I drove my Model A across the desert and back,
and up and down over the hills.

I painted in my studio on wheels—
until the afternoon bees chased me home.

Even in winter,
I went far out into the *faraway*,
and painted in the bitter cold.

I painted when the wind was so strong
it nearly blew me away.

I did things other people don't do.
I climbed my ladder to the night sky
to wait for the sun.

I slept under the stars
to see the morning sky when I woke.

I stayed in the desert.
My hair turned from black to gray
to white as white as the bones.
I still walked the red hills.

My pile of bones grew,
my flowers bloomed in the desert,
and the Pedernal was mine.

And the sky—oh, it was still wonderful!
I painted the sky one more time.
I painted my sky BIG,
so people would see the sky the way I did.

I worked from dawn to dusk every day
for weeks and months.

Then, as I painted the last cloud,
the sun slipped behind the Pedernal.
I laid my brushes down.

Kiss the sky for me. . . .

Georgia O'Keeffe lived to be ninety-eight years old.
In museums all across the land, people see her flowers,
deserts, hills, cities, and skies the way she did.